WORLD CULTURES in Perspective

Brazilian Cultures
IN PERSPECTIVE

ORDEM E PROGRESSO

Tammy Gagne

Mitchell Lane
PUBLISHERS
P.O. Box 196
Hockessin, Delaware 19707

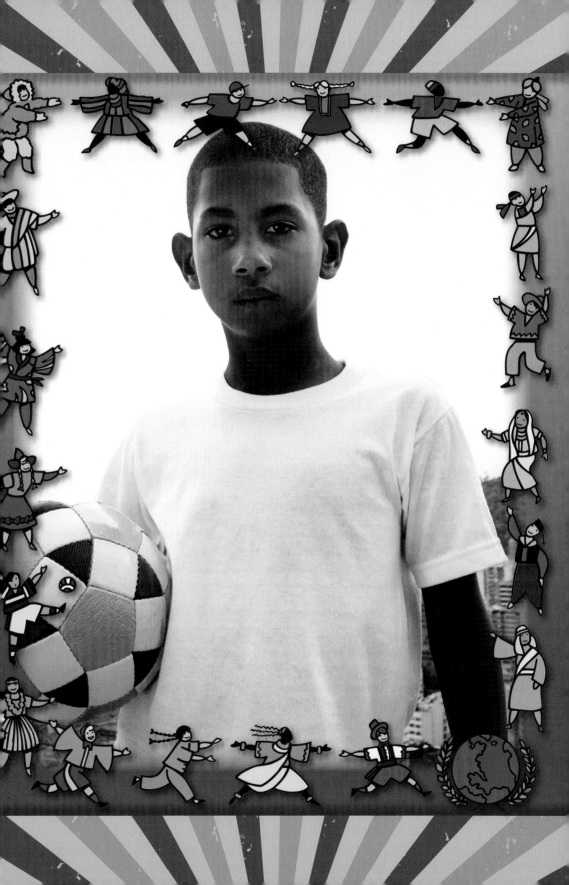

Printing   1   2   3   4   5   6   7   8   9

Library of Congress Cataloging-in-Publication Data
Gagne, Tammy.
 Brazilian cultures in perspective / by Tammy Gagne.
    pages cm. — (World cultures in perspective)
 Includes bibliographical references and index.
 ISBN 978-1-61228-560-3 (library bound)
 1. Brazil—Social life and customs—Juvenile literature. I. Title.
 F2508.5.G34 2014
 981—dc23

               2014020460

eBook ISBN: 9781612285993

PUBLISHER'S NOTE: This story is based on the author's extensive research, which she believes to be accurate. Documentation of this research is on pages 59–61.

The Internet sites referenced herein were active as of the publication date. Due to the fleeting nature of some web sites, we cannot guarantee they will all be active when you are reading this book.

To reflect current usage, we have chosen to use the secular era designations BCE ("before the common era") and CE ("of the common era") instead of the traditional designations BC ("before Christ") and AD (*anno Domini,* "in the year of the Lord").

PBP

CONTENTS

INTRODUCTION

Occupying the northeast section of South America, Brazil is one of the most diverse regions in the world. The country, which makes up about half of South America, includes magnificent beaches, huge rainforests, and lively cities. Brazil is home to numerous ethnicities—including Portuguese, Afro-Brazilians, and indigenous peoples. The people, along with their individual and joint histories, provide the nation with a wealth of cultures. Some have merged together, while others exist almost entirely independent from the rest.

When many people outside of Brazil think of this country, they immediately associate it with soccer, or as it is known in Brazil, *futebol* (foo-chee-BAHL). Many Brazilians see the sport as a significant part of their national identity. The country's national soccer team has won five World Cup championships.

People from all over the world travel to Brazil every year. Many of them go to Rio de Janeiro to celebrate Carnival. This festival can be found in other parts of the world as well, but the Brazilians have the biggest—and many people insist, the best—music, food, and costumes. Brazilian fashion designer Patricia Bonaldi explains, "The Carnival in Rio isn't just fun, with lots of dancing and singing, but is also an important part of Brazilian culture. Everyone has to do it once in their lifetime."[1]

But for all its beauty and fun, Brazil is also a place where problems like crime, discrimination, and poverty run rampant. As the nation moves forward, its leaders are working to make Brazil a safer and more prosperous place for all its citizens. The Brazilian people also hope to preserve their unique cultures along the way.

The opening ceremony of the 2014 FIFA World Cup in São Paulo, Brazil

CHAPTER ONE
A Country Divided

Brazil is one of the largest countries in the world in both geographical size and population. Its two hundred million people occupy more than three million square miles (eight million square kilometers).[1] But what makes this South American nation stand out the most are the people themselves—and their vast cultures.

The moment you begin speaking with a Brazilian, you immediately notice something different. While most of the citizens of other South American countries speak Spanish, in Brazil the official language is Portuguese. The Europeans discovered Brazil more than five hundred years ago. No one knows for certain whom the first person to land on Brazilian shores was. Many people say it was Portuguese diplomat Pedro Álvares Cabral, who commanded a fleet of ships originally bound for India. Others insist Brazil was discovered by Duarte Pacheco Pereira, who wrote about being in Brazil two years before Cabral landed there. Whomever the true first European to claim the South American land was, however, it is certain that he was from Portugal.

Many people credit Portuguese explorer Pedro Álvares Cabral with discovering the South American region now known as Brazil.

The Portuguese were not, however, the first people to live in Brazil. Long before they found Brazil, it was the home of many native tribes. The first tribe the Portuguese met was the Tupinamba Indians.

When the Portuguese first colonized the area, they quickly noticed the large number of *pau-brasil* trees—trees of red wood that were especially useful for making a dye. It was in fact this species of tree that gave Brazil its name. At first the Europeans worked with the native tribes to harvest the trees. Soon, though, the Portuguese had cleared most of the trees in the coastal regions. Once this had happened, some of the colonists moved farther from the ocean in search of other forested areas they could clear. But most of the Portuguese stayed behind.

Without the pau-brasil trade to make them money, these colonists needed a new way to make a living. Sugar plantations would fill this need. The colonists needed people to work on these farms, so they tried to force the native tribes to perform the labor. But this proved to be a poor plan. Many of the natives had died from diseases brought to the area by the Europeans. And most of the ones who survived fled far from the coast to avoid being forced into slavery by the plantation owners.

The Portuguese, like so many Europeans who had colonized the Western World at this time, decided to find their slaves elsewhere: in Africa. Today Brazil's population includes the descendants of the Portuguese colonists, the African people they enslaved, and the native tribes. Many modern-day Brazilians have

Brazil was named for the pau-brasil trees that were so abundant in the area when Portuguese colonists settled there. Although the outside of the tree has a reddish hue, the color on the inside is even deeper red.

a mix of these races in their family trees. The native population has declined immensely since the Europeans first arrived in the country, however. What was once three million[2] is now just eight hundred thousand.[3]

Brazil declared its independence from Portugal in 1822. And near the end of that century, the country would abolish slavery. But even today, the various cultures do not always live peacefully with one another. Writer Jenny Barchfield states, "Many Brazilians cast their country as racial democracy where people of different groups long have intermarried, resulting in a large mixed-race population. But you need only turn on the TV, open the newspaper, or stroll down the street to see clear evidence of segregation."[4]

The racial divide between Brazil's citizens separates the country by more than location. As Barchfield sees it, "In Brazil, whites are at the top of the social pyramid, dominating professions of wealth, prestige, and power. Dark-skinned people are at the bottom of the heap, left to clean up after others and take care of their children and the elderly. . . . Nearly all TV news anchors in Brazil are white, as are the vast majority of doctors, dentists, fashion models, and lawyers. Most maids and doormen, street cleaners, and garbage collectors are black." Racial inequality can also be seen in politics. In Brazil, Barchfield notes, "There is only one black senator and there never has been a black president, though a woman, Dilma Rousseff, leads the country now [in 2013]."[5]

Many of the poorest people in Brazil live in the *favelas* (fah-VEYH-lahs). These are shantytowns, or what people in the United States might call slums. About eleven million Brazilian people live in these and other deprived areas.[6] Expatriate Elliot Rosenberg, who moved to Brazil from Los Angeles, California, also lives in one of these regions. Despite their reputation for crime, Rosenberg insists that the favelas have something important to offer people who are willing to give them a chance.

African slaves played a large part in the early development of Brazil. While Portuguese colonists owned the sugar plantations, it was the slaves who did most of the work.

"I moved because Rio is the most beautiful big city in the world and to start my travel business here. As CEO and founder of Favela Experience, I help provide authentic homestays and apartment rentals for travelers in Rio de Janeiro's favelas, now-safe urban communities with vibrant culture."[7]

Rosenberg admits that people have to be smart about safety. "The city is safe if you're educated about the security of certain places at certain times. You can't carelessly wander around here like in many Western cities. [But] I feel safer in certain favelas than I do in some of the more touristy neighbourhoods such as Lapa and Copacabana, especially at night."[8]

Rosenberg finds "The culture is relaxed, amicable, and fun-loving compared to most work-centric Western cultures . . ." and "the natural setting is unparalleled—bustling beaches amidst lush forests and vertical, rocky peaks. It also never gets cold! Finally, the fruits and juices here are spectacular. . . . You'll taste flavours you didn't know existed." He urges, "Give the favelas a chance, try the *açaí* [ah-sahy-EE; a fruit that grows on palm trees in Brazil], and wear sunscreen!"[9]

Undoubtedly, one of Brazil's biggest natural resources is its wondrous Amazon rainforest. This vast forest covers parts of the South American countries of Brazil, Bolivia, Colombia, Ecuador, Guyana, Peru, Venezuela, and Suriname—as well as the French territory of French Guiana. The Amazon contains 1.4 billion acres of dense forestland. It makes up more than half of the tropical forestland left in the world today.

The Amazon River, the second-longest river in the world, flows through this region. With many tributaries, the waterway measures about 4,000 miles (6,400 kilometers) in length. The lush landscape of the Amazon rainforest offers an ideal environment for numerous life forms. The plant and wildlife contained in the Amazon is as abundant as the land it covers. One in ten of the known species on earth are found within this enormous area.

Recently scientists have begun to worry about the future of this important natural resource. Because the trees of the Amazon hold so much carbon—about 90 to 140 metric tons—the rainforest plays a key role in maintaining our global climate. Deforestation, a practice begun in the area when the Europeans first landed in the region, releases the carbon stored by the trees into the atmosphere. This carbon insulates the earth, causing an increase in temperatures. Changing weather patterns, melting ice, rising sea levels, and the loss of habitats for animals can all result from these carbon emissions. If we do not make great efforts to preserve this region, the effects on our environment could be devastating.

The international crisis has brought attention to the region. But the tribes that live there already know the importance of preserving their cultures—and of protecting the land as well. In 2012, five hundred tribes from different parts of the world gathered together in Rio de Janeiro to discuss these issues. They signed a pact that outlined possible solutions to support biodiversity and limit climate change.

Favelas have a bad reputation for being crime-ridden areas. But some people see these poor neighborhoods as an important part of Brazilian culture. The people do not focus all their energy on work and material riches. Instead, they enjoy the natural landscape, the native foods, and the warm weather.

Chief Biraci Yawanawa led the ceremony. He is also the leader of the Yawanawa tribe, whose members reside in the Amazon rainforest. "We have much to learn from the Western world and they can learn from us," he said. "Our youth has benefited from the education present in cities, but we also want Brazilians to know more about our ancient culture and the importance of preservation through mutual respect."[10]

Mauro Lacombe is the programme coordinator at the Instituto Guardioes de Floresta (IGF). This Brazilian company creates books, films, and cultural exchanges that educate the masses about the wisdom of the various indigenous tribes. Interestingly, their knowledge often proves to be more helpful than many modern strategies for creating sustainability. "Due to the 'un-sustainability' of our current way of life on the Earth," Lacombe asserts, "it is time we rethink our actions as part of a global transition towards a new consciousness. It is time to establish alternative ways of living and relating to each other and the planet."[11]

The Amazon is one of the most populous regions on Earth—in terms of plants and animals, that is. The rainforest is home to forty thousand plant species and more than five thousand bird, amphibian, fish, and reptile species.

True Progress

It may seem that technology is a natural enemy of the environment. After all, it appears that the more we invent, the more ways we destroy our planet. But the members of an indigenous tribe in Brazil suspected that the world's many gadgets could prove to be helpful in the fight to save the rainforests. In 2008, Chief Almir Naramagoya Surui extended an invitation to the Google Earth Outreach team. His area had long been dealing with the problem of illegal logging. He and his people wanted to know how they might work to save their land and culture by using tools like Picasa, YouTube, and Blogger.

Upon their visit to the region the next year, Rebecca Moore and her Google Earth Outreach team taught the tribe how to use the Open Data Kit for Android phones. The members could use this app on their phones to record various types of data, including photographs of the illegal activity.

The chief hopes to pass on what he has learned to others by opening a center for technology and culture on his tribe's land. Instead of working against technology, he wants to show others how modern tools can be used to preserve their way of life.

Illegal logging is one of the biggest problems the Amazon rainforest faces. The Brazilian government is trying to crack down on the offenders by sending its armed forces into the Amazon to stop them.

CHAPTER TWO
Brazilian Religions

More than half of Brazil's population—130 million people—are Roman Catholic.[1] The religion has been the most common in the area since the sixteenth century, when it was brought to the region by the Europeans. And although Protestants now make up a sharply increasing minority, Brazil is still home to more Catholics than any other country in the world.

When Pope Francis was elected in 2013, the people of South America rejoiced. He was, after all, the first pope from Latin America despite its overwhelming Catholic population. The people of Argentina, Pope Francis's native country, were especially pleased, as were many Brazilians.

As part of the new pope's first trip outside of Italy, he visited Brazil in July 2013. President Dilma Rousseff hosted a welcoming ceremony for the leader. Her words were hopeful but candid. "We know that in you, we have a religious leader who is sensitive to the yearnings of our people for social justice, and for opportunities for all. We struggle against a common enemy: inequality in all its forms."[2]

Easter Mass in the Cathedral Basilica in Salvador, Bahia, draws a large number of people each year. More than 130 million people in Brazil belong to the Roman Catholic faith. It was brought to the region by the Portuguese colonists who settled in the area several centuries ago.

Even Brazil's younger citizens were excited to see the Catholic leader. Isabel Cristina Santos de Carvalho was just seventeen years old at the time. "I just had to come and show my adoration," she said. "Francis is with us at all times, but today he's actually in my country."[3]

Brazilian bank manager Cleyton Terto isn't Catholic. He is an evangelical Christian. But he too was among the people who flocked to downtown Rio hoping to catch a glimpse of the new pope. Terto also wanted to snap a photo of the pontiff for his wife, who *is* Catholic. "This pope makes me sympathize more with the Catholic Church than I have in a long time . . . he's closer to the people, more human."[4]

When Pope Francis made his historic first trip to Brazil, people—both Catholics and non-Catholics—traveled great distances to see him. Here, hundreds of thousands gather to listen to his final mass of the trip in Rio de Janeiro. Some of them slept on the beach the night before to help ensure their spot.

Following his visit to Brazil, Pope Francis spoke about his experience there. "The goodness, the hearts of the Brazilian people, are big, really big. They are a very lovable people, a people who like to celebrate, who even amid suffering always find a path to seek out the good somewhere. And this is good: they are lively people, and they have suffered greatly! The liveliness of the Brazilians is contagious, it really is!"[5]

When European settlers arrived in South America, they wanted to replace the religions of the native tribes with their own faiths. Catholicism in particular would ultimately become the major religion of the Brazilian people. But something unexpected happened when the Europeans began transporting African slaves to the continent. These people who were forced to leave their homes with virtually none of their belongings brought something far more important than any tangible item. They brought their own beliefs.

Portuguese plantation owners forbade the slaves from practicing their own faiths. Instead, they insisted that the Africans convert to Catholicism. Some of them did. But others merely pretended to do so, continuing to practice their own religions in secret. As the Europeans introduced them to their Catholics saints, Africans paired each saint with one of their own spirits. While the plantation owners thought the slaves were praying to the saints, they were actually practicing their traditional religions.

Today these hybrid religions are known by several different names—Candomblé, Umbanda, and Quimbanda are the most common. But mention these names in certain circles and you may notice a negative reaction. This is because many people associate these African religions with black magic.

Umbanda has existed in Brazil since the early 1900s. It includes a mix of traditions from West African spirit religions, indigenous beliefs, and Catholicism. It was even influenced by the teachings of a nineteenth-century French spiritualist named Allan Kardec.

Allan Kardec

19

Augusto Prates is an Umbanda medium. He shares that some of his fellow Brazilians have accused him of worshiping the devil. A few have even thrown rocks at his temple. "People think that 'Umbandistas' do voodoo, magic, so you can have success in love and finance. And it is not about this. It's about something beyond. It is about helping," he explains.[6]

At eighty-nine years old, Rose Cardoso has practiced Umbanda almost all of her life. But the entire time, she has kept it a secret from those outside the temple she runs. The temple itself wears a disguise of sorts. Unlike the Catholic churches one finds in Rio de Janeiro, Cardoso's temple has no sign. Even on the inside, a person wouldn't know the building is an Umbanda temple. Figures called *Orixás* (oor-ee-SHAHS), which are symbols of the religion's African gods, are put away when not in use. Instead, one sees images of Jesus and the Virgin Mary at the altar.

"We used to have to hide in the woods to do our ceremonies," remembers Cardoso.[7]

Today some Brazilians try to pin crimes on followers of the Afro-Brazilian religions, saying that they committed them after being possessed by evil spirits. Henrique Pessoa is a police officer in charge of a new office in Rio de Janeiro. The unit investigates crimes of religious intolerance. He agrees that the followers of Afro-Brazilian religions have been mistreated more than members of other groups. "They have been discriminated against since they came here because of their practices and the belief that they were cults," adding that about 97 percent of the religious-intolerance crimes in his area are against Umbanda and Candomblé followers.[8]

Laws that prohibit religious discrimination have existed in Brazil since the middle of the twentieth century. But for many years they were not enforced. Pessoa reports that since the creation of his unit, however, the number of religious intolerance crimes has decreased.

Today about four hundred thousand people practice Umbanda openly. But it is likely that many more Brazilians practice Afro-Brazilian religions in private. One of them is Edmilson Fereira, who was raised Catholic. "I hide the fact that I go to an Umbanda temple because it's criticized, not just by my family but by my . . . friends and co-workers," he says.[9]

Fernando Altemeyer is a theologian at the Catholic University of São Paulo. He explains, "Umbanda has suffered a lot of pressure from other religions, as well as from the state and from police. It has these elements from Catholicism, but isn't Catholic; from spiritualism, without following exactly Kardec's beliefs. So no one recognizes it as their own."[10]

The statue of Christ the Redeemer is the second largest statue of Christ in the world today. Standing at the summit of Mount Corcovado in Rio de Janeiro, it measures 98 feet (30 meters) tall and is 92 feet (28 meters) wide from one hand to the other.

Jewish Brazilians

Many people are surprised to learn that Brazil has a significant Jewish population—over one hundred thousand Jews live in Brazil today, mainly in São Paulo and Rio de Janeiro. Even more surprised are the Catholic Brazilians who find out that their ancestors were Jewish. But clues have existed for many generations in the customs of certain families. For example, many Brazilians have been taught to sweep dust out the back door instead of the front one, as the latter way was thought to bring bad luck. In addition, abstaining from eating pork, praying on the first day of a new moon, and burying dead bodies without caskets are all practices which have their roots in Judaism.

Photographer Elaine Eiger and journalist Luize Valente directed a documentary film titled *The Star Hidden in the Backlands*. It tells the story of the descendants of Portuguese Jews who came to Brazil in the early 1500s. Many of these Jews kept their faith a secret to avoid being returned to Portugal. The Portuguese law at this time stated that all Jews must convert to Catholicism. Those who did not were expelled from the kingdom, tortured, or killed.

Joao Medeiros was raised in the Catholic faith. But for the last thirty years he has been practicing Judaism. When he was a child, his parents would not let him tell anyone about his Jewish ancestry. Now in his seventies, Madeiros states, "I have refused to convert to Judaism—something Brazilian rabbis insist upon—because I am already Jewish. And I have helped create a religious community in Natal that is keeping our Jewish traditions alive."[11]

Former Brazilian President Luiz Inácio Lula da Silva is seen here (left) at Etz Chaim synagogue in São Paulo, Brazil. He attended a special service held on the first International Holocaust Remembrance Day on January 27, 2006.

CHAPTER THREE
Blending Cultures, Music, and Dance

Music and dance have been an important part of Brazilian culture for centuries. As each new group came to the area, the people brought their culture's music and dance customs with them to their new home. Many styles have remained largely unchanged over time, while others have evolved along with the nation itself. Some styles have even influenced modern music and dance, both in Brazil and around the world.

Perhaps the best-known type of Brazilian music and dance—and one of the most popular throughout the world as well—is samba. Samba was developed in Brazil by former African slaves and their descendants. When slavery was abolished in 1888, many former slaves moved from rural areas into the cities. Samba was being performed in Rio de Janiero by the early twentieth century. But it would be another decade or two before samba would find a larger audience. When Brazil's first radio stations were created, people both near and far began discovering the lively music. Its popularity just kept rising from that point forward.

American Elisa Phillips has always loved to dance, but when she found samba, she was instantly attracted to it. "When I traveled to Brazil in 2004 is when I felt a connection to the culture and dance," remembers Phillips. "But I actually didn't start dancing right after my trip, since I was very involved in salsa dancing at the time. One of the dance schools in San Francisco had a samba class, so I dropped in—and the rush I felt when I was in Brazil came back."[1]

Phillips encourages others to learn samba, whether they have dance experience or not. "Learning to samba dance is so much fun, however it did take me weeks just to get the basic step right. It may have been because I threw myself into an advanced class thinking, I know how to dance, I'll pick it up quickly. If you are a natural dancer and understand movement and choreography you will be fantastic. If you think you have two left feet, take a beginner class and just have fun. It's really about enjoying the music and the energy."[2]

Another type of music with deep roots in Brazilian culture is bossa nova. But instead of samba's high-energy dance rhythms, this music style is softer and much more relaxing. Interestingly, bossa nova developed from samba. But it focuses more on the melody of the music than on drumming and fast-paced beats.

Musician Lisa Ono was born in Brazil. Although she moved from São Paulo to Japan as a young child, the music of her native land remained a large influence in her life. Today the multicultural

Singer Lisa Ono is seen here performing during the 2013 Shanghai Jazz Festival in China.

Samba isn't performed only at parties and dance clubs. Many schools train samba dancers to perform in elaborate shows and competitions. Here, dancers from one of Rio de Janeiro's schools perform in the 2004 Carnival parade.

star travels between Asia and South America, known in the East as the "queen of bossa nova."

"Bossa nova was born in Rio de Janeiro, Brazil," explains Ono. "The Brazilian people are a very happy and spontaneous people who love football [soccer] and samba, but at the same time when they look at the beautiful seas and mountains at the end of the day, they feel like relaxing and singing to their lovers in the romantic bossa nova style." Many of Ono's fans outside Brazil also enjoy this soothing musical style. "The delicate sound of bossa nova makes Japanese people very relaxed—well, not only the Japanese people, but especially them. In this fast-going world, we all need to be relaxed," she adds.[3]

When asked which country she considers her home, Ono offers, "I left Brazil when I was ten, but after I turned twenty I started to go to Brazil, and I feel both countries are my home. There are so many differences, but like the yin and yang—it completes myself as one." Bossa nova too bridges the gap between the continents. As Ono puts it, "Bossa nova is the north and the south, the east and the west."[4]

Many people who like Brazilian music find that they also enjoy one of Brazil's most fascinating pastimes: capoeira (kap-oo-AIR-uh). Not quite a dance—yet very much like one—capoeira combines music with martial art. Whenever the martial art is performed, it is accompanied by music created by the group. The movements of capoeira match the rhythm of these songs, providing an especially entertaining experience for spectators. In fact, capoeira is less about a competition between the participants and much more about the performance itself.

Created by slaves, capoeira was a way to disguise their martial art practice from their owners. Soon after slavery was outlawed, capoeira became illegal as well. Officials believed that the people who were performing capoeira were also involved in criminal activity. Still, people practiced capoeira behind closed doors. One especially good capoeirista and teacher was known as Mestre Bimba. Bimba wanted to open an academy to teach others, so in 1937 he performed for the president of Brazil. President Getulio

A group of capoeiristas put on a show outside the Arena Amazonia Stadium just before a match between the USA and Portugal in the FIFA 2014 World Cup. In the background, members of the group play long bow instruments called *berimbaus* (behr-eem-BOUS, center) and hand drums called *pandeiros* (pun-DEY-rohs, right).

Vargas liked it so much that not only did he make capoeira legal, he also wanted to make it a national sport!

Known now as Mestre Camisa, José Tadeu Carneiro Cardoso grew up on a farm in Brazil. He discovered capoeira as a child and learned more about it from his brother. "My brother Camisa Roxa went to Salvador to study, and there he met some capoeiristas and went to train in Mestre Bimba's academies. During his vacations from school, he would come back to the farm and teach my cousins, my other brothers, and me what he had learned. Once he took me to Salvador and I had the pleasure of meeting Mestre Bimba for the first time. I felt all of his force. I was fascinated by watching his students train."[5]

Despite being so young at the time, Mestre Camisa knew right away that he wanted to study capoeira himself. "When I went back to the farm, I was even more motivated and I began training in the corral, doing flips over the manure pile. I did backflips on the riverbank. Everyone in my family was learning capoeira. After my father passed away, my family moved to Salvador and my mother continued taking care of the farm. I went to live in Liberdade, the largest black neighborhood and one of the greatest capoeira centers of all time in Salvador."[6]

Capoeira is much more than a sport to Mestre Camisa. "My life philosophy is capoeira," he says. "I have played since I was a child; capoeira has grown inside of me. My way of seeing the world is through capoeira, which taught me to respect others, to know that we are all equal regardless of social condition." Today he teaches others what he has learned through capoeira. "It enabled me to have a profession with which I completely identify, and I am free to act, think, and develop my work in the way that I think best. I have never had another profession and I wouldn't even want to do anything else."[7]

The Politics of Punk

Much of the music for which Brazil is known has been around for over a century. But many more modern music genres have carved out important spots in Brazilian culture over the past several decades. One of them is punk.

Fernanda Terra is the drummer for a popular Brazilian punk band called Kombato. She explains how politics have affected the music—and vice versa. "A long time ago, Brazilian musicians had to worry about being more censored because there was a brutal military dictatorship. Today, we have made progress and lyrics are not as indirect and don't have to be as metaphorical as they once were. People are bolder. . . . Some bands stray away from [politics], but many, especially punk bands, use the stage to revolt against the current political policies and seek justice. The more and more underground you go, the more political it gets. The more raw the material is."[8]

Terra shares that Brazilian punk culture differs greatly from one part of the country to another. "Some areas are more rural, while others more urban. For instance in São Paulo, there are some real punks (and not just people in bands with tattoos), but kids holding people at gunpoint and stealing cars. There's extreme poverty and people doing what they need to survive. There's a big movement here of people standing up to the government. But like everywhere else, the punks are seen as a minority. There's still some progress to be made."[9]

Poverty is a problem that often leads to crime in Brazil. Many of the poor live in favelas like this one in São Paulo.

Carnival!

Brazil is just one of many countries that celebrate Carnival. This five-day celebration—known as *Carnaval* (kar-nah-VOWL) in Portuguese—includes parades, music and dance, and countless colorful costumes. But nowhere is this lively celebration bigger or more exuberant than in Brazil. Carnival takes place each year in February or March, just before the Christian period of Lent begins on Ash Wednesday. Carnival began as a religious event in Europe. Over time, though, it became a massive block party of sorts celebrated by Christians and non-Christians alike. In Brazil, the largest celebration is in Rio de Janeiro, but there are festivals in most of the major cities.

Nanny Kammura is a kindergarten teacher who takes part in the celebration each year as a samba dancer. "We're here honoring that culture, our roots. It's ours, it's Brazilian. . . . Samba is the root that binds Brazilian culture," she says. "Yes, it's a party. But it's also us honoring our history and ensuring that samba will never die."[1]

Although the dancing is fun to watch, many participants take it quite seriously. In Rio de Janeiro, for example, twelve different samba schools compete against one another in the parades. More than 2,500 people take part in these processions which cost more than $3 million in all. Dancers are judged in ten categories, and a winner is selected near the end of the celebration. The winners receive only a title. But that is more than enough to inspire them— and to delight the spectators.

Zelma Freitas, an office secretary, says that the festivities are worth all the time and effort. "It's pure joy, mostly for those of us from humble backgrounds, who take pride in and root for our favorite [samba] schools," she explained. "Perhaps it's inexplicable to outsiders, but this means so much to the poor, who for the rest of the year have to face our daily reality. Today, I leave that behind and embrace this fantasy."[2]

Brazilian musician Flavia Coelho has fond memories of winning the top samba spot. "I was seventeen when my neighbourhood samba school Grêmio Recreativo Escola de Samba Unidos do

The 2014 Carnival celebration included some spectacular costumes, like these soccer-inspired outfits at the Samba Schools Parade in São Paulo.

Viradouro won Carnival Champions of Rio de Janeiro in 1997. There were thousands of us in the streets of my neighbourhood Niterói celebrating. It was so emotional for everyone because it was the culmination of a year's hard work. For us in Rio, the samba schools are not only a celebration of the historical heritage of the city but they also represent the heart of Brazil, which leaps every time a *bateria* [the percussion section of a samba band] sounds at the Sambadrome."[3]

Samba isn't the only type of dancing done at Carnival. Joyce Moreno is another Brazilian musician. Known to her fans by just her first name, she points out, "Most people think samba when Carnaval comes to mind, but *marchinhas* [mahr-SHEEN-yahs] are also very popular, especially in Rio de Janeiro. Musically, it is similar to a marching band rhythm, but faster, played by a snare drum, and then horns and all the rest. But the most notable aspect of the marchinha is the lyrics, which are comments about everyday life, and facts, usually very funny, ironic, and politically incorrect—but it's Carnaval, so, who cares? Marchinhas date from the 1930s but they're still very popular and played in street *blocos* [Carnival's neighborhood street parties] and Carnaval balls today. There is a big marchinha contest that happens every

Flavia Coelho is from Rio de Janeiro but now lives in France. Her unique blend of samba and reggae music has become popular throughout the world.

year at Fundição Progresso [a big venue in Rio de Janeiro] where new marchinhas are presented."[4]

Despite all the excitement and fun, though, a more serious side of Carnival exists. Brazilian musicians Iggor Cavalera and Laima Leyton explain, "There is a mixture of happiness and sadness which we feel during Carnaval. Brazilians love to party and to celebrate life in every manner, and we try to bring this into everyday life. However during this time of the year people in Brazil also become numb, forget their responsibilities, and appear sedated by the media's vision of Carnaval. A lot of people spend the whole year working for Carnaval for very little or no reward, and then for the rest of the year poverty and corruption carries on. 'A Felicidade' is a popular song at Carnaval because it expresses the short happy moments Brazilians experience, through its lyrics, melody, and arrangement."[5]

Each year a huge Carnival celebration takes place in the center of São Paulo, Brazil.

Carnival: Did You Know?

- Although the celebration was considered a Catholic festivity, its roots actually go as far back as the ancient Greeks and Romans, who held large parties each year to mark the beginning of spring.
- During the 1500s, the Portuguese settlers in Brazil celebrated Carnival with some surprising customs. They would throw mud and "fragrant limes" (balls of wax filled with scented water) at one another.
- More than five hundred street bands play music for the crowds during Rio's Carnival alone each year.
- The celebration brings about two million people into Rio de Janeiro's streets each day.
- Each year, Rio de Janeiro appoints a man to reign over the Carnival festivities as *Rei* (King) Momo. Rio de Janeiro's mayor marks the beginning of Carnival by passing a giant gold and silver key to Rei Momo.
- Rio's largescale parades aren't the only Carnival celebrations. Smaller parades called blocos also take place in various parts of Rio. Some draw thousands of onlookers.
- Carnival celebrations also take place in Olinda, Manaus, Porto Alegre, Recife, São Paulo, and Salvador.
- Rio de Janeiro's Carnival can create as many as 250,000 temporary jobs each year for Brazilians.
- Carnival ends each year on "Fat Tuesday," the day just before Lent begins.

Rio de Janeiro Mayor Eduardo Paes (right) helps kick off Carnival in 2014 with a long-held tradition. He awards a giant key to the city to Rei Momo (center), a traditional character of Brazilian culture. The event is played out again each year to start the five-day celebration.

CHAPTER FIVE
On the Ball

Sports enthusiasts from all over the world will travel to Brazil in 2016 as Rio de Janeiro hosts the Summer Olympics there. The country's second-largest city, Rio is already a popular tourist destination. The city also hosted the 2014 FIFA World Cup™ Final. As exciting as the Olympic Games are, the World Cup is a much more personal one for many Brazilians. Soccer, or futebol as they call it, is the most popular sport in Brazil. And its enthusiasts take the game quite seriously. The nation's 2014 World Cup loss to Germany was especially tough for many Brazilians.

The last time Brazil lost the World Cup to another country on its own turf was in 1950. Few people expected the Brazilian team to lose the game against Uruguay for the World Cup title that year. Angelo Mendes de Moraes was mayor of Rio at the time. Shortly before the fateful game on July 16, he congratulated the Brazilian players just a little too soon. "You, players, who in less than a few hours will be hailed as champions by millions of your compatriots!" he announced over the loudspeaker at the Maracanã, the world's biggest soccer stadium. "You, who have no rivals in the entire hemisphere! You, who will overcome any other competitor! You, who I already salute as victors!"[1]

Of course, the team's loss was made all the more painful by the mayor's—and the other fans'—certainty that their beloved national team simply could not lose. Following the loss, many of those fans held grudges over the defeat. They especially blamed Moacir Barbosa, the goalie who had been in the net.

Barbosa said that his performance in that single game followed him for the rest of his life. Once when he was shopping in a grocery store, a woman recognized him. As soon as she realized who Barbosa was, she told her young child how the man in front

Many Brazilians wouldn't let goalkeeper Moacir Barbosa forget the 1950 World Cup loss—not that he could forget if he tried. Everyone was certain that Brazil would win, but Uruguay ended up winning the match against their hosts with a final score of 2 to 1.

of them had disgraced Brazil. Neither the child nor the woman herself had even been born when Barbosa had played in the 1950 World Cup. But she had heard the story nonetheless.

In 1994, more than four decades after the World Cup loss, Barbosa showed up at a practice for that year's national team. He wanted to watch the players practice and wish them well in the upcoming event. The team's coach had only been a teenager when the Brazilians lost in 1950. But he had been taught that Barbosa was bad luck. And he clearly believed it. He wouldn't allow him to speak to the team.

In an interview toward the end of his life, Barbosa suggested that he had been punished worse than a criminal for losing the game for Brazil. At seventy-nine years old, he said, "Under Brazilian law the maximum sentence is thirty years. But my imprisonment has been for fifty years."[2]

In the years following the 1950 loss, Brazil redeemed itself on many international soccer fields. Some of the best players in the sport have hailed from the South American nation. Without a doubt the most famous is Pelé. Since he first played in the World Cup in 1958, he has become a cultural icon in his home country. He is the only person who has ever won three World Cups—in 1958, 1962, and 1970. Tarcisio Burgnich had been the defender matched against Pelé in the 1970 game. Burgnich later confided to the press, "I told myself before the game, he's made of skin and bones just like everyone else. But I was wrong."[3]

Looking back on his first World Cup, Pelé said, "I was too young; it was like a dream. After scoring in my first game, I gained confidence and thought, 'My God, now I can stay in the team.' Then against France I scored three and when we came to the final, it was like a dream too. I didn't have much experience and no responsibility because I was the youngest. It was something unreal—very different to my last World Cup. In 1970, the emotion and responsibility made it a totally different experience."[4]

National Public Radio host Melissa Block traveled to Brazil in 2013 to see firsthand the country's preparations for the 2014 World Cup. "It'll be the first time Brazil has hosted the Cup since 1950,"

The Brazilian team celebrate their 1994 World Cup win against Italy. The finalists played the deciding game at the Rose Bowl in Pasadena, California. The game ended in a shootout with a final score of 3 to 2.

she noted on the air. "And if you ask Brazilians to name all the years their country has won the World Cup, it's on the tip of their tongue. . . . Brazil is five-time World Cup champion. No other country can say that. I went to Maracanã for a club game this past weekend and even with just nineteen thousand fans, it was rocking."[5]

Block was joined on the radio by Carlos Alberto Torres. As captain of the Brazilian national team, he won the World Cup in 1970. He explained, "Football—soccer—in Brazil, is like a religion. Everybody wants to be a soccer player."[6]

41

Although he hasn't played competitively in decades, Pelé remains one of the best known soccer players in both Brazil and the rest of the world. He is seen here at the 1970 World Cup Final match in Mexico City against Italy. Brazil won that game with a final score of 4 to 1.

Alex Bellos is the author of *Futebol, The Brazilian Way of Life*. He also lived in Brazil while he wrote for *The Guardian* newspaper. As he explained to Block, "Brazilian football is unique because it is what united the nation like nothing else. . . . It's just part of what it is to be Brazilian. You can't sort of opt out. It's part of what you are."[7]

Bellos compared the way Brazilians play the sport to the way they do other physical things in their culture. "It embodies a certain way that you move your hips and it's exactly the same as if you were to go and look at a samba dance . . . or capoeira. . . . There is something about the way that Brazilians move. They dribble better. There's more flamboyance, they're kind of showing off. They evolved this incredibly kind of creative, fun way of playing football. And by complete coincidence, it turns out that it was really successful."[8]

Dave Chesler is US Soccer's director of coaching education. Like Block had done earlier, Chesler traveled to Brazil in 2014. But his biggest goal was to find out what American players can learn from the Brazilians. "It was invaluable," he said of his trip. "The passion and the way the sport is woven into their culture is amazing. I think a large part of the learning experience was confirming that we do many things right in this country in terms of player development. The other side is also confirming their passion, structure, and organization are well engrained in their society and the development of players is at a much higher level than it is here right now."[9]

Some players have made their way from Brazil to play for the United States. A few years after his 1970 World Cup win, Pelé was one of them. In 1975, the New York Cosmos paid him $2.8 million to play for the team for three years. Although he had retired from playing the sport in Brazil by then, he was still going strong. Many people credit him with truly introducing the sport of soccer to the United States fans. In just those three years, attendance at games increased by a whopping 80 percent. He led his American team to a championship before he retired for good in 1977.

Yan Gomes plays for the Cleveland Indians in the United States. Although he came to the US from Canada's Toronto Blue Jays, Gomes began his baseball career in Brazil.

Leading the Way

In 2012, Yan Gomes became the first Brazilian baseball player to make it into the major leagues. After playing for the Toronto Blue Jays for a single season, he joined the Cleveland Indians. Soon he would become the team's starting catcher. He would also prove to be a talented hitter. With a batting average of .294 in 2013, he hit 11 home runs in 88 games.

Baseball isn't nearly as popular in Brazil as it is here in the United States. But that didn't stop Gomes. As soon as he discovered the sport through a friend of his father, he was hooked. "It was kind of weird going to school and telling people that I played baseball," he admitted. "They had no idea what it was. But I fell in love with the game at a young age."[10] Indeed, he had already been playing for six or seven years when he moved to Miami, Florida, at the age of twelve.

Gomes knew the best way to increase his opportunities on the field was to play a number of positions well. Now a scout for the Blue Jays, Kevin Cash is a former catcher. He noticed Gomes's versatility immediately when he started watching him play. "He was all about playing third, playing first, catching, whatever he could," remembered Cash. "He just volunteered to do everything, and he always did something positive to impact the game."[11]

Gomes hopes to introduce more Brazilians to baseball. But in the meantime he is pretty happy with being a bit of a pioneer in the sport. He is already featured in the National Baseball Hall of Fame and Museum in Cooperstown, New York. The cap and jersey he wore in his very first MLB game are on display at the museum. "Being the first guy from such a huge country known for their athletics," he acknowledged, "it's pretty nice."[12]

45

CHAPTER SIX
A Taste of Brazil

Whether celebrating Carnival or simply enjoying time with family, food plays a large role in Brazilian culture. And like the rest of Brazil's culture itself, its cuisine is made up of many different flavors. In the northeast area of the country, seafood is extremely popular. A love of seafood comes from the Portuguese settlers who brought salt cod and dried shrimp to the region. But many dishes in the northeast are also made with Afro-Brazilian ingredients like coconut and coconut milk, palm oil, okra, and peanuts. Head south and you will notice more dishes made up of meat, rice, and beans.

Brazil has many acclaimed restaurants. Alex Atala is the chef at a restaurant called DOM (Deo Optimus Maximus). Located in São Paulo, the establishment was voted the seventh-best restaurant in the world in 2014 by The Diners Club® World's Fifty Best Restaurants Academy. He wants all of Brazil to be known for its delicious cuisine. "We are so proud of our soccer, our models, our music, our graffiti artists. Why is no one excited about Brazilian food? Brazilian food is so amazingly diverse, and we have to celebrate that."[1]

Atala explains that part of preparing food in Brazil is cooking for large numbers of people. "We don't cook for one, we cook for ten," he says.[2] And he's not just referring to the restaurant business. Some of the most popular dishes in the country are *paneladas* (PAHN-ey-lah-duhs). These are dishes cooked in a single pan for a large group of people. Common ingredients include coriander, dried beef, and burnt garlic.

Brazilian fashion entrepreneur Daniela Cecilio points out that DOM serves "Brazilian food with a cool twist," and "Chef Alex Atala sources wild ingredients from Amazonian tribes and uses them in inventive, delicious ways."[3]

Brazilian chef Alex Atala thinks Brazilian food—like its music and soccer—should be celebrated.

Atala too has his favorite restaurants. "I love young chefs who source their ingredients locally," he shares. His favorite places include Mani in São Paulo, which offers "wonderful outdoor dining rooms and delicious food," and Remanso do Bosque in Belem do Pará "which feels like a bit of the Amazon within the city." He also likes Trindade in Minas Gerais "which offers real variety, from octopus appetisers to Portuguese-style desserts" and Banzeiro in Manaus "in the heart of the Amazon, which has a small, perfectly curated selection of Brazilian flavours."[4]

Isabeli Fontana is a supermodel in Brazil. Her favorite place to eat is Pelô Bistrô in Salvador. "Its patio overlooks lush gardens: the perfect spot for lunch or a romantic dinner. I almost always have *bobo de camarão* [BOH-boh jee kam-er-AOW]: pureed shrimp with coconut milk, flavoured with palm oil," she shares.[5]

Marcos Antonio Gouvêa learned how to cook from his parents while growing up in Brazil. Now a professional chef, he lives in New York City. He states, "Brazilian cuisine is very rich, thanks to the country's fertile earth and other natural resources; it's also a reflection of Brazil's diversity and, dare I say, joy of life. I don't think it can be compared to any other international cuisine although it certainly has been influenced by culinary traditions from all over the world. . . ."[6]

Gouvêa credits the intensity of Brazilian food to the native ingredients. "The richness of Brazilian cuisine is obvious in the wide array of flavors, colors, and especially aromas in dishes from around the country, and because of its unique ingredients including yucca, dende oil, corn, tapioca, and bulgur wheat, that when combined with staples such as beef, chicken, seafood, pork, rice, and beans, produce culinary magic. And I haven't even mentioned fruits like mango, passion fruit, papaya, pineapple, and even more exotic ones from the Amazon, all common in our cuisine."[7]

Jennifer Torrey teaches an international cooking class in Santa Rosa, California. Among the Brazilian dishes she instructs her students to make are *vatapá* (vah-tah-PAH), a spicy seafood stew, and *feijoada* (fay-ZWAH-da), a dish made of pork and beans and usually served over rice. One of her most popular recipes of late has been *pão de queijo* (pow jee KAY-zhew), a gluten-free cheese bread made from tapioca flour. "I think most people are coming for the bread," Torrey admits. "Everyone has either had it or heard of it."[8]

The bread, like many other dishes from Brazil, came from the country's African slaves. At first Torrey had a hard time finding the tapioca flour used in the recipe. But because so many people have changed to gluten-free diets, more stores now carry it. The Africans

Pão de queijo

Papaya and mango

added cheese to the recipe to add to both the flavor and texture of the bread.

Feijoada too can be traced back to slave kitchens. Beans were an inexpensive ingredient for meals. And the pork was added when the plantation owners gave the slaves leftover parts of their pigs that they didn't want to eat themselves. Today both the rich and the poor alike enjoy the dish in Brazil.

Vatapá comes from Salvador, Bahia. Yoruban slaves from West Nigeria brought their method for preparing this dish with them to

Brazil. Different cooks prepare it different ways. But the stew is most often made with chiles, coconut milk, ground nuts, and palm oil. "I like to make it sweet and spicy," Torrey shares. "It's very, very simple and quick. Being a stew, it's a good thing to eat here in the winter."[9]

One of the best parts about the meals Torrey teaches her students to make is that they are so authentic. When she worked in the wine industry, she traveled extensively. "I was invited to stay in the homes of the distributors," she points out. "This was the real food that people ate at home."[10]

Brigadeiros **are sweet chocolate treats that are popular throughout Brazil. The fudge-like candies are usually coated with chocolate sprinkles for a crunchy outer layer. Home cooks make them for special occasions like holidays and birthdays.**

Breaking Bread

In 2013, a group of University of Chicago students gathered at a Brazilian restaurant called Sinhá to learn about the country's culture. In the four hours they were there, they also got a chance to practice their Portuguese. They were hosted by Jorgina Pereira, the owner of the restaurant where they all met up.

Ana Lima is senior lecturer and Portuguese language coordinator at the University of Chicago. She spoke highly of the experience—and of the restaurant owner herself. "Jorgina was very warm and very welcoming, and she volunteered a lot of information. After two questions, she had given us her life story."[11]

Liz Margolis was a second-year student who took part in the trip. "The Brazilian culture is very similar to those of other Latin American

Chicago is home to a large community of Brazilian immigrants. Instead of leaving their culture behind, these warm, upbeat people brought their culture to Chicago. Here, Brazilians in Chicago celebrate the news that Rio de Janeiro was selected to host the 2016 Olympic Games.

countries, very giving and open," she shared. "I learned that Brazilian people are very relaxed. They go with the flow, and they're very happy."[12]

Katherine Jinyi-Li was a senior when she attended. She added, "The culture is one of hospitality, immense love for Brazil, and nostalgia. Through the way she explained the food, it was clear that Jorgina has a great love for her country, and the way that her home is set up shows that she is all about sharing her love for Brazil." She noted that she didn't realize there was such a large Brazilian immigrant population in the United States. "Seeing someone go through that journey and learning why she left was an amazing experience. I now see that Brazil is a place that can be manifested in Chicago."[13]

Experiencing Brazilian Culture in the United States

If you can't make it to Brazil, but still want a taste of Brazilian culture, don't worry! There are plenty of ways to experience the culture of Brazil right here in the United States!

Carnival
Carnaval Brasileiro in Austin, Texas, was first formed in the 1970s by Brazilian students studying in the area: http://sambaparty.com/

Events
Many cities host Brazilian events and festivals, often featuring live music and dance performances and authentic foods and crafts.

Brazilian Day in New York City is held at the end of summer each year
http://www.brazilianday.com/en/

Brazilian Day Philadelphia, each year in September
http://www.braziliandayphiladelphia.com/

Brazilian Fest in Pompano Beach, Florida, each year in November
http://www.brazilianfestpompano.com/

Brazilian Summer Festival in Hollywood, California
http://www.braziliannites.com/

Restaurants
Boteco, Miami, Florida: This restaurant serves authentic Brazilian cuisine, and even offers free samba classes on Monday nights!
http://www.botecomiami.com/

Cafe Brazil, Denver, Colorado, http://www.cafebrazildenver.com/

Brazilian Steakhouses
Green Forest Churrascaria, Penn Hills (Pittsburgh area), Pennsylvania
http://greenforestdining.squarespace.com/home/

Rodizio Grill (multiple locations), http://www.rodiziogrill.com/

Fogo de Chão (multiple locations), http://www.fogodechao.com/

Dance and Capoeira
SambaLa, Long Beach, California, http://www.sambala.org/main/

Quenia Ribeiro, dance instructor in New York City
http://www.sambany.com/?lg=en

CapoeiraList, find capoeira classes near you, http://capoeiralist.com/

Online Radio
Brazilian radio stations, http://www.live365.com/genres/brazilian

Bossa Nova, http://www.sky.fm/bossanova/

Film
Los Angeles Brazilian Film Festival in September
http://www.labrff.com/

Brazilian Film Festivals (summer in New York and Miami)
http://www.brazilianfilmfestival.com/index_en.html

Map of Brazil

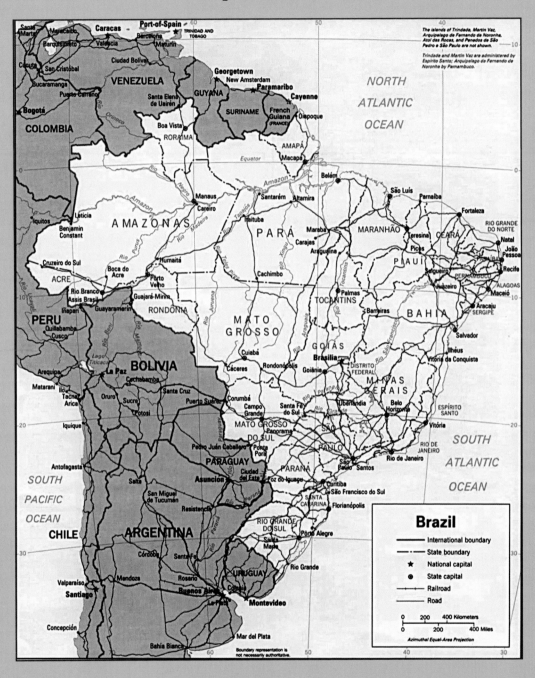

TIMELINE

Early 1500s	Portuguese explorers land in Brazil.
	Portuguese settlers celebrate Carnival in Brazil.
1822	Brazil declares independence from Portugal.
1888	Slavery is abolished in Brazil.
1892	Capoeira is outlawed in Brazil.
Early 1900s	Brazilians start performing samba in Rio de Janeiro.
1942–1945	Brazil joins the Allied Forces in World War II.
1950	Brazil loses the World Cup to Uruguay.
1958	Brazil wins the World Cup against Sweden.
1962	Brazil wins the World Cup against Czechoslovakia.
1970	Pelé becomes the only person to compete in three World Cup victories.
1977	Pelé retires.
1992	The Earth Summit is held in Rio de Janeiro.
1994	Brazil wins the World Cup against Italy.
2002	Brazil wins its fifth World Cup against Germany.
2004	Brazil requests a permanent seat on the United Nations Security Council.
	Brazil launches its first space rocket.
2005	Voters reject a referendum to ban the sale of firearms.
2008	Chief Almir Naramagoya Surui invites the Google Earth Outreach team to his village.
	Brazil rejects Iran's invitation to join the international oil cartel, OPEC.
2011	Dilma Rousseff becomes Brazil's first female president.
2012	Yan Gomes becomes the first Brazilian baseball player in the major leagues.
2013	Pope Francis, the first Latin American pope, is elected. He visits Brazil in July.
2014	Brazil hosts the World Cup.
2016	Rio de Janeiro hosts the Summer Olympics.

CHAPTER NOTES

Introduction
1. *UltraTravel*, "The Fashion Set's Guide to Brazil," Winter 2013, pp. 38-39.

Chapter 1: A Country Divided
1. Central Intelligence Agency, *The World Factbook*, "Brazil," April 29, 2014. https://www.cia.gov/library/publications/the-world-factbook/geos/br.html
2. José Fonseca, Fodors.com, *New York Times*, "A Brief History of Brazil." http://www.nytimes.com/fodors/top/features/travel/destinations/centralandsouthamerica/brazil/riodejaneiro/fdrs_feat_129_9.html?n=Top%2FFeatures%2FTravel%2FDestinations%2FCentral+and+South+America%2FBrazil%2FRio+de+Janeiro
3. Central Intelligence Agency, *The World Factbook*, "Brazil," April 29, 2014. https://www.cia.gov/library/publications/the-world-factbook/geos/br.html
4. Jenny Barchfield, *Huffington Post*, "Race in Brazil: Majority-Minority Nation Offers Lesson to U.S.," March 17, 2013. http://www.huffingtonpost.com/2013/03/17/race-in-brazil-offers-lesson-to-us_n_2895325.html
5. Ibid.
6. "Direito à Moradia Adequada," *Síntese de Indicadores Sociais* (Rio de Janeiro: Instituto Brasiliero de Geografia e Estatística, 2012), p. 220.
7. Globe Media, ExpatArrivals, "Interview with Elliot Rosenberg—An American Expat Living in Brazil," June 2013. http://www.expatarrivals.com/article/interview-with-elliot-rosenberg-an-american-expat-living-in-brazil
8. Ibid.
9. Ibid.
10. Preethi Nallu and Zack Embree, *Al Jazeera*, "The Amazon's Keepers Reach Out to the World," July 16, 2012. http://www.aljazeera.com/indepth/features/2012/07/2012714205050912413
11. Ibid.

Chapter 2: Brazilian Religions
1. Central Intelligence Agency, *The World Factbook*, "Brazil," April 29, 2014. https://www.cia.gov/library/publications/the-world-factbook/geos/br.html
2. Vincent Bevins and Tracy Wilkinson, *Los Angeles Times*, "In Brazil, Thousands Turn Out to Greet Pope Francis," July 22, 2013. http://articles.latimes.com/2013/jul/22/world/la-fg-pope-brazil-20130723
3. Ibid.
4. Ibid.
5. The Vatican, "Press Conference of Pope Francis During the Return Flight," July 28, 2013. http://www.vatican.va/holy_father/francesco/speeches/2013/july/documents/papa-francesco_20130728_gmg-conferenza-stampa_en.html
6. Somer Wiggins, *Ottawa Citizen*, "Umbanda Followers Worship Despite Prejudice; Brazilian Spirit-Focused Religion Seen as a Cult," July 8, 2012.
7. Associated Press, *Bennington Banner*, "Century-Old Afro-Brazilian Religion under Threat," December 15, 2011.
8. Somer Wiggins, *Ottawa Citizen*, "Umbanda Followers Worship Despite Prejudice; Brazilian Spirit-Focused Religion Seen as a Cult," July 8, 2012.
9. Ibid.
10. Associated Press, *Bennington Banner*, "Century-Old Afro-Brazilian Religion under Threat," December 15, 2011.
11. Michael Kepp, JTA, "Documentary Looks at Brazilians Rediscovering Their Jewish Roots." The Jewish Federations of North America, May 25, 2005. http://www.jewishfederations.org/page.aspx?id=74955

Chapter 3: Blending Cultures, Music, and Dance
1. Laura Cococcia, *The Journal of Cultural Conversation*, "Global Samba: Interview with Elisa Phillips," September 5, 2009. http://www.thejcconline.com/global-samba-interview-with-elisa-phillips/
2. Ibid.
3. Simon Smith, *That's Shanghai*, "Interview: Lisa Ono, the Queen of Bossa Nova," February 10, 2014. http://online.thatsmags.com/post/interview-lisa-ono
4. Ibid.

CHAPTER NOTES

5. Shayna McHugh (translator), *Capoeira Connection*, "Interview with Mestre Camisa," October 27, 2011. http://capoeira-connection.com/capoeira/2011/10/interview-with-mestre-camisa/
6. Ibid.
7. Ibid.
8. Andrea Jackson, *Suburban Apologist*, "The Whirling Girlish: Interview with Brazilian Drummer Fernanda Terra," November 12, 2013. http://www.suburbanapologist.com/the-whirling-girlish-interview-with-brazilian-drummer-fernanda-terra/
9. Ibid.

Chapter 4: Carnival!
1. Bradley Brooks, *The Gazette* (Colorado Springs, Colorado), "Brazil Keeps up Carnival Pace of Parties, Parades," March 3, 2014.
2. Ibid.
3. Lewis Robinson, *The Guardian*, "The Songs That Make Brazil's Musicians Think of Carnival," February 28, 2014. http://www.theguardian.com/music/musicblog/2014/feb/28/the-songs-that-make-brazils-musicians-think-of-carnival
4. Ibid.
5. Ibid.

Chapter 5: On the Ball
1. Joshua Robinson, *Wall Street Journal*, "The Defeat That Brazil Can't Forget," November 4, 2013. http://online.wsj.com/news/articles/SB10001424052702304682504579154172398189230
2. Ibid.
3. Gentry Kirby, ESPN Classic, "Pele, King of Futbol." http://espn.go.com/classic/biography/s/Pele.html
4. John Naughton, *GQ British*, "When GQ Met Pelé," February 24, 2012. http://www.gq-magazine.co.uk/entertainment/articles/2012-02/24/pele-interview-football
5. Melissa Block, NPR News, "In Brazil, Soccer Is a Way of Life," September 20, 2013. http://www.npr.org/2013/09/20/224514655/soccers-place-in-brazilian-culture
6. Ibid.
7. Ibid.
8. Ibid.
9. USSoccer.com, "Q & A: US Soccer's Director of Coaching Education Dave Chesler Discusses His Role and What's Ahead." http://www.ussoccer.com/news/coachesnet/2011/04/dave-chesler-interview.aspx
10. Tyler Kepner, *International New York Times*, "First Brazilian in Majors Hopes He Is a Trailblazer," February 25, 2014.
11 Ibid.
12. Ibid.

Chapter 6: A Taste of Brazil
1. Jenny Barchfield, *The Times* (Munster, IN), "Discovering Brazil's Cuisine: Chef Hopes to Introduce World to His Food," October 30, 2013. http://www.nwitimes.com/lifestyles/food-and-cooking/discovering-brazil-s-cuisine-chef-hopes-to-introduce-world-to/article_04ace664-85cd-5608-9a52-6bef0d824f2a.html
2. Mina Holland, *The Telegraph*, "Carnival Cuisine: Brazilian Recipes," March 3, 2014. http://www.telegraph.co.uk/foodanddrink/10668380/Carnival-cuisine-Brazilian-recipes.html
3. *UltraTravel*, "The Fashion Set's Guide to Brazil," Winter 2013, pp. 38-39.
4. Ibid.
5. Ibid.
6. Rodrigo Brandão, BrazilNYC, "Exclusive Interview with Acclaimed Brazilian Chef Marcos Antonio Gouvêa," January 20, 2013. http://brazilnyc.com/brazil-on-the-table/
7. Ibid.
8. Diane Peterson, *The Press Democrat*, "Carnaval Cuisine," February 25, 2014. http://www.pressdemocrat.com/article/20140225/lifestyle/140229764
9. Ibid.
10. Ibid.
11. Sarah Miller, Chicago Studies, "Sinhá Restaurant Offers a Taste of Brazilian Food and Culture to Students Learning Portuguese," June 7, 2013. https://chicagostudies.uchicago.edu/features/sinh%C3%A1-restaurant-offers-taste-brazilian-food-and-culture-students-learning-portuguese
12. Ibid.
13. Ibid.

FURTHER READING

Books

Bellos, Alex. *Futebol: The Brazilian Way of Life*. New York: Bloomsbury, 2014.

Farah, Fernando. *The Food and Cooking of Brazil*. Leicestershire, UK: Anness, 2012.

Hale, Lindsay. *Hearing the Mermaid's Song: The Umbanda Religion in Rio de Janeiro*. Albuquerque: University of New Mexico Press, 2009.

McGowan, Chris, and Ricardo Pessanha. *The Brazilian Sound: Samba, Bossa Nova, and the Popular Music of Brazil*. Philadelphia: Temple University Press, 2008.

Roberts, Yara Castro, and Richard Roberts. *The Brazilian Table*. Layton, UT: Gibbs Smith, 2009.

On the Internet

AllRecipes: Brigadeiro (Brazilian chocolate candy)
    http://allrecipes.com/recipe/brigadeiro/
Brazil Carnival Videos (YouTube Channel)
    https://www.youtube.com/channel/UCnvlcPWxdAVF5OgcfEMhp5A
Capoeira Group in Salvador, Bahia, Brazil
    https://www.youtube.com/watch?v=6H0D8VaIli0

Works Consulted

Associated Press. "Century-Old Afro-Brazilian Religion under Threat." *Bennington Banner*, December 15, 2011.

Barchfield, Jenny. "Discovering Brazil's Cuisine: Chef Hopes to Introduce World to His Food." *The Times* (Munster, IN), October 30, 2013. http://www.nwitimes.com/lifestyles/food-and-cooking/discovering-brazil-s-cuisine-chef-hopes-to-introduce-world-to/article_04ace664-85cd-5608-9a52-6bef0d824f2a.html

Barchfield, Jenny. "Race In Brazil: Majority-Minority Nation Offers Lesson to U.S." *Huffington Post*, March 17, 2013. http://www.huffingtonpost.com/2013/03/17/race-in-brazil-offers-lesson-to-us_n_2895325.html

Bevins, Vincent, and Tracy Wilkinson. "In Brazil, Thousands Turn Out to Greet Pope Francis." *Los Angeles Times*, July 22, 2013. http://articles.latimes.com/2013/jul/22/world/la-fg-pope-brazil-20130723

Block, Melissa. "In Brazil, Soccer Is a Way of Life." NPR News, September 20, 2013. http://www.npr.org/2013/09/20/224514655/soccers-place-in-brazilian-culture

Brandão, Rodrigo. "Exclusive Interview with Acclaimed Brazilian Chef Marcos Antonio Gouvêa." BrazilNYC, January 20, 2013. http://brazilnyc.com/brazil-on-the-table/

Brazil Carnival. "Origins of Carnival." http://www.brazilcarnival.com.br/culture/orgin-of-carnaval-r-history-of-word-carnival

Brooks, Bradley. "Brazil Keeps up Carnival Pace of Parties, Parades." *The Gazette* (Colorado Springs, Colorado), March 3, 2014.

Central Intelligence Agency. "Brazil." *The World Factbook*. April 29, 2014. https://www.cia.gov/library/publications/the-world-factbook/geos/br.html

FURTHER READING

Cococcia, Laura. "Global Samba: Interview with Elisa Phillips." *The Journal of Cultural Conversation*, September 5, 2009. http://www.thejcconline.com/global-samba-interview-with-elisa-phillips/

Fonseca, José. "A Brief History of Brazil." Fodors.com, *New York Times*. http://www.nytimes.com/fodors/top/features/travel/destinations/centralandsouthamerica/brazil/riodejaneiro/fdrs_feat_129_9.html?n=Top%2FFeatures%2FTravel%2FDestinations%2FCentral+and+South+America%2FBrazil%2FRio+de+Janeiro

Fox, Zoe. "Android Phones Help Brazilian Tribe Save Amazon Rainforest." Mashable, June 8, 2012. http://mashable.com/2012/06/08/android-brazil-rainforest/

Globe Media. "Interview with Elliot Rosenberg—An American Expat Living in Brazil." ExpatArrivals, June 2013. http://www.expatarrivals.com/article/interview-with-elliot-rosenberg-an-american-expat-living-in-brazil

Holland, Mina. "Carnival Cuisine: Brazilian Recipes." *The Telegraph*, March 3, 2014. http://www.telegraph.co.uk/foodanddrink/10668380/Carnival-cuisine-Brazilian-recipes.html

Jackson, Andrea. "The Whirling Girlish: Interview with Brazilian Drummer Fernanda Terra." *Suburban Apologist*, November 12, 2013. http://www.suburbanapologist.com/the-whirling-girlish-interview-with-brazilian-drummer-fernanda-terra/

Jornal Cidadania. "Does Carnival Belong to the People?" March 31, 2011. http://www.fundacaobunge.org.br/en/jornal-cidadania/news.php?id=7327&/does_carnival_belong_to_the_people

Kepner, Tyler. "First Brazilian in Majors Hopes He Is a Trailblazer." *International New York Times*, February 25, 2014.

Kepp, Michael. "Documentary Looks at Brazilians Rediscovering Their Jewish Roots." JTA, The Jewish Federations of North America, May 25, 2005. http://www.jewishfederations.org/page.aspx?id=74955

Kirby, Gentry. "Pele, King of Futbol." ESPN Classic. http://espn.go.com/classic/biography/s/Pele.html

McHugh, Shayna (translator). "Interview with Mestre Camisa." *Capoeira Connection*, October 27, 2011. http://capoeira-connection.com/capoeira/2011/10/interview-with-mestre-camisa/

Miller, Sarah. "Sinhá Restaurant Offers a Taste of Brazilian Food and Culture to Students Learning Portuguese." Chicago Studies, June 7, 2013. https://chicagostudies.uchicago.edu/features/sinh%C3%A1-restaurant-offers-taste-brazilian-food-and-culture-students-learning-portuguese

Nallu, Preethi, and Zack Embree. "The Amazon's Keepers Reach out to the World." *Al Jazeera*, July 16, 2012. http://www.aljazeera.com/indepth/features/2012/07/2012714205050912413

Naughton, John. "When GQ Met Pelé." *GQ British*, February 24, 2012. http://www.gq-magazine.co.uk/entertainment/articles/2012-02/24/pele-interview-football

FURTHER READING

Peterson, Diane. "Carnaval Cuisine." *The Press Democrat*, February 25, 2014. http://www.pressdemocrat.com/article/20140225/lifestyle/140229764

Ramón, Paula. "Poor, Middle Class Unite in Brazil Protests." CNN, July 24, 2013. http://www.cnn.com/2013/06/28/world/americas/brazil-protests-favelas/

Robinson, Joshua. "The Defeat That Brazil Can't Forget." *Wall Street Journal*, November 4, 2013. http://online.wsj.com/news/articles/SB100014240527023 04682504579154172398189230

Robinson, Lewis. "The Songs That Make Brazil's Musicians Think of Carnival." *The Guardian*, February 28, 2014. http://www.theguardian.com/music/musicblog/2014/feb/28/the-songs-that-make-brazils-musicians-think-of-carnival

Shoichet, Catherine E. "First Latin American Pope 'Very Exciting,' Faithful Say." CNN, March 14, 2013. http://www.cnn.com/2013/03/13/world/americas/latin-america-pope-reaction/

Síntese de Indicadores Sociais. Rio de Janeiro: Instituto Brasiliero de Geografia e Estatística, 2012.

Smith, Simon. "Interview: Lisa Ono, the Queen of Bossa Nova." *That's Shanghai*, February 10, 2014. http://online.thatsmags.com/post/interview-lisa-ono

UltraTravel. "The Fashion Set's Guide to Brazil." Winter 2013, pp. 38-39.

USSoccer.com. "Q & A: US Soccer's Director of Coaching Education Dave Chesler Discusses His Role and What's Ahead." http://www.ussoccer.com/news/coachesnet/2011/04/dave-chesler-interview.aspx

The Vatican. "Press Conference of Pope Francis During the Return Flight." July 28, 2013. http://www.vatican.va/holy_father/francesco/speeches/2013/july/documents/papa-francesco_20130728_gmg-conferenza-stampa_en.html

Wiggins, Somer. "Umbanda Followers Worship Despite Prejudice; Brazilian Spirit-Focused Religion Seen as a Cult." *Ottawa Citizen*, July 8, 2012.

Withnall, Adam. "Rio Carnival 2014 in Numbers." *The Independent*, February 27, 2014. http://www.independent.co.uk/news/world/americas/rio-carnival-2014-in-numbers-brazil-kicks-off-the-greatest-party-on-earth-tomorrow--but-where-will-the-samba-parades-take-you-9157909.html

World Wildlife Fund. "Amazon." https://worldwildlife.org/places/amazon

GLOSSARY

biodiversity (bahy-oh-di-VUR-si-tee)—the variety of different plant and animal species in an environment.

choreography (kawr-ee-OG-ruh-fee)—the art of arranging the movements or steps of dances, usually to match a particular piece of music.

compatriot (kuhm-PEY-tree-uht)—a person from one's own country.

entrepreneur (ahn-truh-pruh-NUR)—a person who starts, organizes, and manages a business, often risking their own money and time.

expatriate (eks-PEY-tree-it)—a person living in a foreign country.

indigenous (in-DIJ-uh-nuhs)—originally living in a particular region or environment.

inexplicable (in-EK-spli-kuh-buhl)—impossible to explain.

metaphor (MET-uh-fawr)—a figure of speech in which a word or phrase meaning one kind of object or idea is used to represent another object or idea.

segregation (seg-ri-GEY-shuhn)—the separation or isolation of a race, class, or group.

sustainability (suh-stey-nuh-BIL-i-tee)—the quality of not being harmful to the environment or depleting natural resources, and supporting long-term ecological balance.

theologian (thee-uh-LOH-juhn)—a person who studies religion.

INDEX

INDEX

About the Author

Tammy Gagne is the author of numerous books for both adults and children, including *We Visit South Africa* and *The Nile River* for Mitchell Lane Publishers. One of her favorite pastimes is visiting schools to speak to children about the writing process. She resides in northern New England with her husband, son, and a menagerie of animals.